Tilt a World

Tilt a World

Certainty Lacks Imagination

Holly Brians Ragusa

Amused Moon

Amused
Moon

Tilt a World
Certainty Lacks Imagination
Published Amused Moon January 9, 2024
HBR Writes 2024

Library of Congress Control Number: 2023922726

All rights reserved   ISBN 979-8-9869156-4-7
Subject Poetry

Printed in the United States of America on Acid free paper

Photography credit and cover art design by Author
Holly Brians Ragusa & HBR Writes

First Printing, January 2024

May we become the history worth repeating.
May we learn. May we learn. May we learn.

Dedicated to complex heads
with uneasy thoughts who resolve to embrace the day.

With grudging and requisite gratitude to our most
commonly tugged at threads and greatest teachers-
Grief, Ego & Time.

ACKNOWLEDGEMENTS

-*Dreamless Sleep* published *LaPiccioletta Barca* [Feb 2021]
-*Truth* published *Substack* [June 2023]
-*Two Candles* -first published in Ohio Poetry Association annual compilation *Common Threads* [2021] and in *Inverse: Informed Thoughts by an Unfit Poet* [Feb 2023]

Deep appreciation to three distinctive and consummate poets; John Burroughs, Jonie McIntire & Mervyn Seivwright -Grateful for the magnanimity & warmth you've wrapped around me in friendship & favor. Sincere thanks also to Chuck Salmons, Pauletta Hansel, Yalie Saweda Kamara, Manuel Iris, Rikki Santer, Patti Niehoff, MoPoetry Phillips, Norman Finkelstein, Sandra Feen, Nik Macioci, Ellen Austin-Li, Stacy Sims, Jason Blakely & Jim Palmirini. Wonderstruck by all the many poets in my beloved Ohio poetry community.

-Also by the author-

Met the End
-An Investigation of the Past, a Daughter's Duty to Herself

Dying to Know Myself In Time

Inverse; Informed Thoughts by an Unfit Poet

CONTENTS

CONTENTS

CONTENTS

CONTENTS

CONTENTS

Life Flips Us Round

Life flips us round.
Dizzy with wonder how our minds go sideways
Spun and undone it's our turn to climb out or strap in.
Since the world got us going
How much have we paid for this ride ?
We paid for this ride, we pay for this ride
How much does it cost?
To stay right in this mind.

Connected

Stay your hand. Do not clear my web,
it is of my making and my life lies in its precious lines
My children will know to return to this place

Their children will not be born in a world torn by our hand
The children that matter to you sleep under my shared sky

Soften your fist. Do not act in fear
though your eyes may not recognize my design
As the geese fly, many directions point to home

Certainty Lacks Imagination

Toddler, I questioned life
Its colors, tastes and textures
Adults answered with ways to name
The world they wished me to see

Child, I questioned life
Its happenings and possibilities
Adults answered with facts wrapped in opinion
Layers my young mind could not peel away

Student, I questioned life
Its philosophies and atrocities
Adults answered in riddles and certainties
Quoting infamous or well meant legends

Young adult, I questioned life
Its misfortunes and shortcomings
Adults answered with explanation and excuse
Nuances my inexperience could not decipher

Parent, I questioned life
Its inadequacies and my own
Adults answered with solutions and statistics

Numbers that count on others' joys and sorrows

Quinquagenarian, I questioned life
Its destructions and constructions
Adults answered with opinion disguised as facts
Confident belief stuffed with agenda and ego

Writer, I question life
Its colors, tastes and textures
I answer with ways to name
The world I wish to see

Caved Woman

These petroglyphs might survive
Caved inside my growth
Under the microscopic lens of myself.
A kaleidoscope spins new truths on a sofa
I once recognized
From a time of man.
Squirming, I repeatedly thrive
And die in the petri dish of my mind
Evolving to know nothing is certain,
Hypothetically.
Man still drags Mother by her hair
Still cast out by a cock or caldron and
Science stews in this pot of melting fact
While truth pours steaming from
This simple colandar
I continually poke holes in
Fogging your vision.

Salish Sea- Mt. Baker from Anacortes, Washington

Shades of Blue

There's no time this morning, in the rush to not be rushing.
Today's calendar is filled with the poet's cause
and cannot accommodate other moods and requests
for bland conversations
while the wonder and weariness of this globe spins in space.

Tomorrow's day is packed -
simpering over simplifications, aching for shared travesty
and brokering injustice on this broken planet.
Tomorrow will cause action and seep sorrow once again.
No shortage of sorrows.

This morning - I'm committed
to contemplate most particular, singular shades of blue.
Shades not even cerulean can trace,
deepening in the depths of a warm ocean that's being painted
on my mind in bold strokes.

Luxuriating lunch-a lapping cyan lagoon
may delight me under the cover of shale clouds.

The afternoon will flatten me
beneath Sherwin Williams matte white ceilings

where, imagining a world accessorized by kindness and twilight,
I'll envision us studded with stars, draped in midnight,
wearing that riot of rich velvet only a winter sky can sink into
when dressing for dinner.

Maybe, before the end of day
I'll entertain aegean and the peace found in sublime saxe
hiding in feathered pelts of an evergreen at nightfall.
Cornflower will accompany me to dinner
considering the tenacious tart of turquoise for dessert.

After I've washed denim soot off the day,
in my bed will lurk the teal-tinged calm of a Scottish loch
ferrying me into azure sleep where glacial skies will
dapple my dreams with snow from yesterday's rain
Oh, painful, bustling world, I've no stomach for my other blues.

Woke

Woke, by no definition that defines this fear flooding my mind
- Floating under life -
A buoy of isolation is far easier to reach than love's shore.

Why won't we swim to those countless grains of possibility?

Currents of certainties shut out an undertow of consideration.
Shame casts us into deep waters.
Yesterdays' lungs suck on sorrow, and tomorrows too tumultuous, lurk deep.

I know the forecast.
My boat may leak if I care to the point of breaking.
Mutiny, to suggest all hands be on deck.

Drowned in the nightmare of losing today, we sleep.
Momentous loss.
Filtered light ticks time, panning for gold through screens.

Slick and cavernous maybes glide by.
And we can hide there, away from care.
Fascinated by other currents, not felt from this shore.

Cannot hide from the nightmares we become in others' dreams.

Waking disconnected.
Emptiness hauls heavy into our boats,
reflecting our tossed selves back in placid waters.

I know the way.
All boats will break without the costly cargo of care.
Safety in our sheets we ignore the beckoning call.

Wake.
We are light housed.
We can burn for others in darkness.

World Builder

What makes my world turn may make yours burn

Only ash will tell those stories

I'm not interested in your version of righteousness
We are not better or worse than each other
We are worlds of hurt with exit ramps

Read and believe what you will,
what steels your resolve and feeds your ego

I'll do the same and build a world where yours
will not crash down on mine

Where love may be inclined to move in with us
in a land we only carpet bomb with kindness

Where your joy is left for you to determine and my joy is mine

Where my fear becomes your problem to solve and your fear, mine

Where stepping into space
is not the only way to alleviate this pain

Sylvan

Masts topped, billowing with green sails,
Trees tack a steady course on a warming wind.
Belowdecks, anchored ancient into seabeds of clay and stone,
Life dwells in core samples rooted into earth. Soiled by purity.

Over, above and aloft. Ever upward, trees climb
Despite our cutting, despite our cutting.
Planted in whatever expanse lives now and next
We take their giving, elemental shelter and shade.
Leafy limbs wrap around our wormy wood
Despise our cutting, leaving empty shadows on a drying earth.
Ancestral roots all, seeded, flash fuel for our fire,
Sylvan we stand, leafed in ligneous lines. Pervasive, invasive.

Devouring a terminal wood. And still we float beneath closed lids.
Eating away at ourselves. Cutting away. Held fast by weighty
Wings that won't free us from our miniature moment here.
And see how one does no harm?
Limbs still wrap around our wormy wood. Beholden, and bound.
Take root in me. My mossy mind grows soft in a hard world.
Cut me down at the feet of ancients. So that I may return.

Towering - Moran State Park, Washington

Manspread

Maya Angelou — *Each time a woman stands up* for *herself, without knowing* it *possibly, without claiming* it, *she stands up* for *all women.*

Trapped in a wheel turning
through this time and mans' fiction
She in me and I spin together with Her
unbroken in this line of brokenness
Circles carry us only so far
without a road to travel
Ceremonial tokens in make believe games
no prizes for women of war
Moved on a board we did not create with our creations
forced on a bed we did not make with our makers
Standing too far from peaceful resolutions
what could a millennia of elected mothers produce

What could a millennia of motivated mothers make
What would happen if women lay claim

What if a millennia of mothers remained
What if a world full of women lay claim

Each inch of manspread's reign
Each ounce of injustice of womanhoods blame

Stories unmade need remaking
silence pierces voices yet sung
My living revives in Her death
my vision sees through all eyes blinded
My reason spreads through legs for my birth
multiplying in our subtractions
Loss will expand a heart or suck it dry of compassion
Mans' drought spreads us too thin
Nurturing this unnatural environment
to have baked bread from crumbs
To have taken seeds and planted soldiers
to have built our enemy's army

Unnatural

Oh, the imperforate beauty of the morning glory
Blue orbs unflinching, peer into an unabashed sun

Shrinking on petals beneath gaseous gaze is the mysterious dew
worlds swirling unto themselves, eliminated

Might I pass my hours in pursuit of petals careening
their marvelous heads to smile upon that fickle sun

Shall I disclose feathery secrets hidden in chittering song
passed between two angels perched on a nearby rail

I long to speak of beauteous things, yet how can I be distracted so,
when, again, history determines my daughter and yours, chattel?

Why do I exist in a skin that wraps itself around me
when insisting I obey another?

What can vigilant eyes praise in a world of possibility
when sobbing for loss of autonomy?

How can We grow open into the sun
when the dark hand of misogyny presses US into shadow?

Who can look to the skies
when deficient and recently laid foundations already crumble?

How can I sing with those birds
when I want to scream?

As a sun sets, petals close around their own beauty.

Perhaps today's sun shines in a window of one loving her choice
asking no forgiveness for stealing mine.

Perhaps our enriched ground
is seeded for disaster.

Perhaps gentle rains were made
to also fertilize the inhumane.

Perhaps the hailstorm taught us
to pillage and plunder.

Perhaps cool breezes will forever blow soft
on the man who raped me and that ilk who reap those harvests.

Running

Inside is dark as a backlit shadow,
flat black and seeping
into overwhelming puddles of too muchness

Only through light does darkness take shape
Goodness rarely arrives without its mate

Both shoulders occupy the heavy weight upon me
What is laden upon you ?
Evil is candy wrapped in shiny paper, swallowed

Do we belong
to this world or not
Won't be answered at Sunday school
Laws were made to teach us to run
From ourselves

Window opens to clouds in
New England

My Attic

Cobwebs catch
on rafters in my mind

Oceans of antiquated thought
boxed in dark depths

Dust mites and my mongrel selves
dance on delicate strands

A time capsule vacuum
where jet streams fight for crawl space

Once alive
now found afloat feckless

Past twilight pearls of possible debut
sunspots in my vision

Disjointed feature films
swirl story

At all angles
until fade out

Forgotten worlds wrap
round newly traveled planes

Wound up tight
I fall through bottoms

Withering on unwieldy webs
with dead dreams to suck life from later

Overheard

FOR THE BOOK...

I decided against the waffle
We are in a bad situation now
It's very scary but she's gotten lucky
She thinks I'm dense
Sun never sets on badass
I wrote a book, you can find it here
You laying there fucked up
Are you gonna put your clothes on Nan
She used everclear
You know how it goes
He's leaving me
Do all kids like celery
I believe in most stuff
It don't matter dumbass
It's just coffee
I grew up in the hills
Are you being facetious

Tease

Earth tilts into her best light.
Shifting smiles through amber glasses
Cooling the sweat of summer's brow

She simmers slowly.

Under limelight and burnt umber,
Softening the squint in our eye,
Sweetly she scatters herself,
Breathless in our ear.
Ablaze in a chill,
Warming to each other,
We walk longer into evening

With the moon.

Shapely trunks boast ruby jewels
Costumed across furrowed necklines.
Once fashionable frocks of emerald are
Brazenly discarded for cloaked sunsets.
Tints of timelessness, shadowed sepia, reveal
An ochre goddesses past her prime.
Earth tones undress slowly,

Tarnished in bronze, festooned in gold.
An artist's palette

Hits the floor

Stunned we stand,
Witness to death's gilded dance,
Circling us in shreds,
Crushing beneath ungrateful feet,
The thinning slip she can no longer bear to wear.

Tree - Calton Hill, Edinburgh, Scotland

Best Girl Friends

Attention-Getter **WOMEN** Bitch Dumb Gold-Digger Slut Cow Fangirl Jealous Blonde Cunt Huge Liar Tease Selfish Bossy It Shrew Baby Smelly **CAN** Uncoordinated Dumpy Fluff Nothing Diva Pussy Tart Witch Floozy Naive Hooker Tramp Foe Flit **LIFT** Spinster Know-It-All Hag Zero Sinister Simple Nerd Hoe Fatty Sweetie Shrew Vixen Siren Broad Mean-Girl Dog Rival **EACH** Clueless Geek Waste-of-Space Chunky Nag Inexperienced Hussy Bitchy Self-Centered Stupid Girly Crude Ugly Prima Dona Pest Bore Prick-Tease Wears-the-Pants Uncool **OTHER** Baby Mama Prissy Wench Two-Faced Harlot Whore Weak Fallen **UP**

Knit

Kindness has touched me
I offer my share

And yet,
Pain is so palatable

Addiction?

Filled awful full
This world is a drain
We swirl down together

And yet,
Beauty is inescapable

Inherent?

I am left with the sneaking suspicion
Things tie together in the end.

Potluck

I grew up thrown together
in glass casserole dishes
spread over ice cream socials.

Fellowship found itself
beautifully bland in basements,
warmed on patios, heated in kitchens.

Nourished without hierarchy,
leftovers left on hungry plates.
Tupperware held us tight with cloth napkins

when experience cradled youth nicely in its arms.
I was fed on the tender bits of yesterday.
Nice isn't normal anymore.

Drop

tip
pit si
tick pit
tok si splat pip
pat pitter pit splat tik
rat Tat rat Tat rat Tat tok si
Tat rat Tat si tift Ting spat splotch
blop! Tat Tat pit pit pit tok tok tip pit
pit pit Ting pat pit pat pat pit blop! splotch
splotch Tat patter tick tift pit pat pit pit pat patter
pit pit Tat rat rat pit pip pit pip blop! patter tik tik tik
plat Plop pit pit pit pit tok tok tok tift tift rat tik pat
splotch pit tok tok tok pit tift patter tift pat tok pip pit
splat Tat tift Tat tick pit tick pit splotch tok spatter tat
pit pit pip pit pit pip blop! Tat pit pit pit pit Ting pip
pip spit tok tok tick pip pit pit pip tok splat patter
tok rat tok rat pit tick Ting plat splat tik splotch
tok tok pip pip pip blop! splotch Tat rat Ting
splotch rat tift tok rat blop! patter tip pit
ting patter splotch Tat rat pip blop!
pip Tat splat splotch tip spat
splat patter pip blop!
splotch blop!

tok
tick tick
pit patter pit
splat tick pit pit
splotch Tat rat tok
splat splat blop! Ting
pat pat tok Ting tok splat
pit pit splat Tat Tat pit rat rat
pip pit pat rat rat rat si Tat pit splat
splotch pit patter pit pip patter pit tift
tok tok rat rat Ting rat rat tok pattersplat
splotch tift blop! tift rat rat splat patter pit
pip pip pat patter pip splat tift pip pip pit
tok tick tok tok tok tok tok rat pip pip pit
splat tick tift splat tick tift tik tok tok rat
splotch Ting blop! splat rat splotch
splat patter pit tift pit tok Tat
Ting tatter rat Tat si plop
tick blop! Tat splat
patter splat

Dropped Things

Dropped a few things in my time
Expectations
A line, and I liked how it sounded
Grades
Relationships for preservation
The leash
Hints
Petty complaints
Money into a hand in need
Tears
Dirt on a coffin
Flowers on a grave
A ball someone else let fall
Glasses, always glasses
A call I never should have answered
A curse word in a crowd
Fights
Hands in frustration
A broom and left the mess
Did I mention expectations
Everything when needed
Still picking up after myself and others

Raised In Sin

Church raised me on a Midwest street
In a Midwest town twice on Sundays
Ministers don't rain hellfire down on us Presbyterians

I sat in that pew
My grandpa did too
The hymnal did wonders
for his aching back
It sometimes feels good to be bad
Raised to feel this guilt that I feel
Sin seeped subtlety in with the collection plate
We ought to feel bad to be good

A string of beads comes with the steeple across town
The Lord's prayer trespassed at 5 o'clock mass
Our debtors served potluck in fellowship hall

Door Number Four

Every night I walk by door number four
the room,
where the womb
that carried me sleeps
and I think what a gift it is
to give her that rest

and to remember that
without her labors
and her love,
and a life of giving that

I would be but a speck
instead of a spark

And my gratitude is immense
and cannot cover this sky
this ground
my core
or the universe
and cannot be measured
by a Mother's love

Death on Friday

For Mom, a beautiful spirit, since 1941, and always.

Mom sat in the chair across, asked if I had some time.

After answers from the agent led her to the family room,
we both agreed life insurance offers no assurances.
You're priceless, I said, can we not stress it?

Mom and I talked about death on Friday.
Not any death.
Her death.
She isn't dying.
Not dying in the immediate sense. Though,
undoubtedly, whether slow or swift, all our timers run out.

Ageism would have us believe her clock will stop sooner,
though it didn't slow Dad's.
My feet have been running five years longer than his ever did.

Six years ago I began asking questions,
taking care to jot down her particulars.
Yes, we are crazy like that,

we make notes on forgone conclusions.
When two years last I checked in,
her song choices were not outdated.

Eight decades and the end of a policy prompted renewed inquest.
Were there any changes to her plans for leaving? We joke.
Final touches to add on to the end of her life?

A simple question.
One too many won't ask.
Death, that fearful unknown, known to all eventually,
sits in a corner shrouded, listening to every word,
unwelcome at every event, last to leave.
Awkward, that necessary invite.

The circle opens and closes and we find ourselves inside it.
Having lived, our bodies, the miracles that they are,
took a first breath and must also have a last.

Mom places her days in her Maker's hands
and is thankful for each one.
The sun rises on her gratitude.
Birdsong and a warm cat in her lap
are the simple joys she counts as greatest treasures.
She is a Queen.

Tested faith assures her another version of this life,
an upgrade, one lasting and heaven sent.
Loves lost here will greet her there.

Beloved grands and parents, a husband,

brother, a favorite dog and maybe even me
will welcome her into everlasting peace.
It's as beautifully believable
as anything else one might believe.
Destination, we know, is only part of the adventure.

And though we may travel by different itinerary and map,
an excursion is coming, one neither of us rushes to meet
or refuses to plan, for the boat will pull us from shore either way.

Traveling documents anticipate
posted signs along the paper trail of a life.
Forgo your power here, leave behind your wealth there,
bequest that family heirloom there.
Leave a message where you're going,
where you've been.

Take your time getting there, if you can.
Fill in the forms, look around, take account of what you have.
Mom again mentions red tape. She gets stuck, dealing with life
dealers.

Paper pushers need to be paid.
Witness, sign, notarize, make formal the accounts.
Help the courts upend regret and greed.
There will be no sibling battles for Mom's crown.
We had time with the real prize.

So we talk. I say there's no problem discussing it
since it won't happen for a hundred years more. Mom laughs.
It's like an umbrella, we won't need it if we bring it.

We feast on the famine of loss.
Death is ever-present, the elephant seen.
For once you've walked with death,
cleaned the mess strewn in its wake,
far greater appreciated is the host who slices
burnt pieces away from grief when it is served.

So a detailed list of notation grows.
New friends added to her list of who to call first, as we confirm
hymns and hydrangeas that will accompany her final passage.

We reexamine the trappings of death,
the personal, the mundane.
What she might wear for her final performance.
What words will celebrate her life.
We scoff and scorn the scam of term life insurance,
high premiums for the known risk of aging.

Greater returns on a well invested life,
we make this memory.
This honest encounter.
Time and a bit of courage
let us experience her full life together,
which will include her death.

My own journey may see me gone first,
My children have my travel plans.

Pére Lachaise Cemetery, Paris, Autumn 2021

Ghost Story

I don't feed on hurt
The way I used to,
when the specter of grief
sucked at my gut and haunted my soul.
When courage fled, signals jammed
and sensibility deserted me.

My heart no longer sinks to the bottom
of deep longing.
My head doesn't run circles around
what might have been.
Wonder won't waste time
asking why hardship happened.

Today's pain reaches for a torch
lit with hope's faint mystery.
Willful it steps into darkness
listening close for hard truths,
navigating uncharted anguish.
In collapsed passages

I am overturning stones.
Today's torment eases me
Into unknown tomorrows
Having met Fear, having seen myself
held in its intimidating eye,
Dream's oracle reminds me

That familiar face will come again.
I lay a table in wait.
Since we share blood
I invite yesterday's ache in to sit for a spell.
With no new news to upset the table,
the day will go about itself.

Pain's story informs my years.
Chapters close and begin anew
at love's beginning, in loss's end.
My sorrow knows its seasons.
And I am no longer haunted by my ghosts

Murmuration

Late summer's starling slashes through
Westward vision

A moment of isolation
Before a winged dancer follows
And another joins in

Still another is pulled to
The sky
A dance floor filling
Swaying synchronous

Aeronauts beating air
in the noisy machine of their murmuration
Dark clouds swirling
Around and against their inevitability

Choreographing a time
When we could unite
Contract and expand in cacophony

When we too might
Mount heated waves and sink into each other

Voluminous

Unconquerable mountains stare down my limits
Oh! To travel the peaks and valleys of those pages
stacked and sprawling before me!

I long to wade in their waving grains
To climb the unassailable, embossed cloth plateaus
Bound in all directions, adventure waiting.

Though unshakable foundations rest beneath my words
Still, a striated historical bedrock lays unearthed.
I cannot journey to every land and name legion authors

Unless time traveled me a thousand lifetimes in books
To remember what I've yet to experience.

To memorize every desirable line
To hear the beat of every heart bleeding onto pulp
With intimate knowledge.

Countless novels and nonfictions, unexplored,
Undisturbed dystopians and unraveled articles,
each lost pilgrimage of page plagues me.

Oh! How I miss the bones of poems I won't suck on,
The meaty pieces of literature left uneaten on my tables.

Tormented by literary phantoms
That will never possess or bedevil me
I'm reading.

I'm aging.
And the eyes are starting to go
And the towering piles grow.

Copious words, faint and desperate, I envision them,
Feasting on that sweet and savory language I'll never taste,
Starving for knowledge lost to me by time.

Dreamless Sleep

Power left these northern hills that summer's eve when sun ceased to set and night became all encompassing day. Summertime eyes would not close for fear of flying into dreams untethered to the natural cycles of darkness and light. Myth and magic ruled over the minds of this starkly draped land. Here it was preached and believed that if one were to slip into the stories of sleep during the daylit night, the soul would freeze inside the nightmare of a parallel world of darkness. Officials and clansmen passed down the decree and every winter hence for months on end, hammers would silence, plows would lay idle and wash lines hung empty as families, now fattened on the harvest, would hibernate in huddles of fur atop hide seeking to find warmth and recapture months of sleep lost. Evergreens, the only life peeking out from the folds of their cold downy blanket, limbs weighed heavy under frozen clouds. Heard on the frostbitten breeze was a quiet song most cavernous. Nothing could disturb winter's slumber.

Spring would welcome depleted forms back to daily rigor and routine, the strongest set to survive. Not even the warming cries of the young could stave off Solstice, terrorized by days with no nights when any meaningful sleep was forbidden. Villagers' eyes once lit from the inside during more temperate months, were dulled to a doll's finish at summertide, a collection of lifeless souls pulled into positions made to look meaningful. Sobbing children of summer, soaked the streets with their tears, too weak to carry their sadness far. Their adults took turns standing watch over them and each other, never questioning the necessity to fight the exhaustive control of their bodies. Protectiveness prevented tired eyes from the deepest landscapes of sleep. Loved ones snatched awake their wives and mothers, husbands and brothers from the clutches of the hills and valleys of rhythmic breath that might ensorcell them away to that foreign land of obscurity. Generations had fed on months of unrest and those lessons taught the townsfolk to dismiss any internal alarms, never to heed calls for change. A public was sworn to their path as wayward as it may be. For how could they ever return to their loved ones if there were no light to see their way home.

Babes of summertime were swaddled and nursed lightly, never fed full. Allowed only moments to close their eyes, newborn breaths deepened, tiny muscles twitched with restful release until their mother's pinches pierced the town with their bruises and wails. Work was as unrelenting as the listlessness that imbalanced their young limbs. Planting was methodically slow, flattened by fatigue, lumbering became a danger to any who wielded an axe without a steady gaze.

Autumn would sink the sun below the horizon and reclaim the life of the residents. Harvest overfed them in readiness for winter. Talk rarely ensued of the battle they'd just waged on themselves and their families, passively enduring the hardship of warring oneself.

As mornings returned at dawn the laborious sounds of sawing and stomping, stitching and stewing, preparation and resignation settled over the town. By fall equinox, bodies hefted and minds had re-learned a right to sleep. Feeding on stories of what must be for what has been, villagers awaited the coming chill.

Children born of Yule were nursed continually, lulled to sleep by the collective hum of the huddled masses. By springtime they knew little else but to eat and sleep, draining mothers of health and concern. As the sun reheated and remade the days, young ones with full bellies who had run off to play could often be found deeply asleep under trees, difficult to wake, further proving the pull of the darkness on the other side of dreams. Prayers and chants were praised and sorcery blamed.

Rituals kept hold of the townspeople, funneling them into ceremonies and practices that encouraged the fear that lived among them. When an adult found sleep, and dreams came upon them, the stupor of being awakened buzzed the body, blurred the vision and tormented the mind. One's own family could see dreamers of summer when awakened were not themselves. After visiting the other world and returning, demonic quality was assigned, penalty of pain promised and such infractions were publicly demonstrated.

Without the bravery to ride out to meet summer's Sleep, that goddess and graveyard of dreams, no rest could soothe the wearied villagers. After decades of fighting within and without, eventually madness split their minds, divided families, and sickness seeped into the town. Winter's darkness devoured poor souls one by one by the first morning of spring, when a lone young mother and her babe peeked out of their folded furs they woke to the rotting lives around them. Body broken by hunger, the young creator cradled her pale child registering the slowing beat of their hearts on their joined march toward death. In her weakness she found her only strength, a soft voice, unwavering in its aim. Singing to soothe, singing to wish her child to sleep.

Reason

Reason sits at odds with a mind
That sinks and soars on power.
Riled into weapons, we rage.

Worlds exist between us.
We don't hear borders except in bombs.
Collapsing, to expand our hearts.

Hidden versions of ourselves have
Forgotten the deeds of our apathy.
Childhood is a war waged on children.

We forget, unforgiven love lives on in hate
Long after we've outgrown all the
Reasons that safety abandoned us.

War of Words

We no longer make room for *and*.
Sides cannot advance an *and* narrative.
Sides are directional, us versus them, either/or. Yours or mine.

Mine, is an isolated incident, a broader concept.
Mine, is reason for war.
And war cannot contain *and*.

This poet declares war on war.
This poem will read mute to an ambitious goal.
These words won't stop a train in its tracks: they only question

Why is convergence catastrophic?
Why must we barrel full steam into each other?
Why must we steer clear?

My life cannot offer peace to others
Even if it wanted to. Few streets are safe.
And after I'm snuffed by too many carbs, a bad heart

Or shot by an angry bullet, pointed by empty choices,
Only then will there be no war.
For one of us.

Until then, I rage on war
While we barrel full steam into each other and argue
The meaning of peace.

Peace cannot be found, it is made in a thousand kindnesses.
Peace is constructed in microscopic moments of restraint.
Peace forms in a heaping helpings of liberty and self awareness.

Peace dwells not in promise, tax break and boundary.
Peace roots in a blade of grass trampled by fading footprints.
Peace insists the path be perpetually tread anew.

Cored

I'm zoned commercial
The mourning doves don't mind
The wires outside my window
Line them up for their day.
If I could fly I wouldn't be walking to work.
Still I'd choose feet over wheels
Considering the cost of parking.

Infrastructure takes cars where they're going.
My taxes take me
Into the school and park next door
And past affordable housing for my neighbors.
I won't complain about helping while being helped.
Broken concrete eventually gets fixed
And we'd all get fixed
If we walked more evenly with one another.

What a World

What a world, what a world we walk in
Weathered on winds of change
Pushed into mountains
High on reaching peaks, conquering majesty

Fed on this remarkable timeshare
Take stock of this treasure
Formed in moonstone and magic
Teeming in the sea, schooled instinctive
We float on a Milky dream, reverent, repentant, ignorant

Timed. Breathe in and out a life
Rouse, in and out, in and out of sleep
Wake to feel, listen to know
Watch and wander
Engage in the possible, await a bloom in winter

Time hides in history, pond bottoms and fur

What a world, what a world we preach in
Steeped in judgement
Forced into boundaries
High on waging war, conquering neighbors

Spilled dark over stars, still we shine
Under prairie grass, we tunnel
Eagle eyed, we nest in a crevice
Sunsets will only scrape the tallest tree
Where light flutters silent as the moth

Lost, even as air roots us in this garden
We blister ourselves harvesting earth
Ice bakes under northern light
Our timelessness is insanity raining in a desert
Watering yesterday's storm

We are found hiding in yesterday's storm

What a world, what a world we learn in
Step in awe
Journey this jungled gym
High on life, conquering fears

Ownership

Yesterday Israel welcomed a babe in a manger
Today it turned away a hermit in a cave
Environmental protections they say.
Fifty years overturned, a home unlearned
Apparently you may not own your knowledge
without expensive paper. Certified.
Do plagues better prepare us for purpose?

Money has no appetite for lowly houseboats.
On the Nile, Docs with high bank rank, and
Dollars always make better sense of evictions.
Interest rates and inflation now live in houses
Politicians and Billionaires declared tents unl-awful

If we are made in God's image, why aren't we born with coin?
Pray to almighty development to erase the sky with a high rise
and be sure to leave your square footage better than you found it.
This Waste. A. Way. game only deals in concrete gestures.

Darn fish won't recognize our boundaries.
Land, is not allowed to allow pioneers while Nature,
far too generous for her own good, fetches a pretty tax penny.
Long term visitors be aware, you'll need a decal to visit this earth
Stay as long as you pay for this planetary park.
Notice posted - Can't ride here for free.

July 2022- Israeli Ministry of Environmental Protection moves to evict him the hermit Nisim, who in 1974 built, by hand, a Gaudi-like structured house in Herzliya Israel by the sea using recycled and natural materials.

July 2022- The Egyptian government forcibly evicts residents of houseboats permanently docked on the banks of the Nile river, in Giza.

September 2022- Animals trapped and anglers in Colorado cannot fish public rivers due to Billionaires' fences and claims.

No Country Girl

I'm in a land of plenty

    of inches
        imprisoning grams

    and here
        we are great at this transaction

Plus and minus
filling voids
pumping holes

    depositing us nonsensically

        into micro states

                of mind

    take account

my phone passively pings military time
investing in twenty-four

saving all the hours

    withdrawing from this glaring sun

  depositing me elsewhere

under other shadows

over one nation

                living

beneath slivers of moon I won't see

    seeing light

someone else and their flag

    loves to gaze beneath

Oil Tanked

The ground swells with richness
billions of heartbeats drumming
rhythms priceless

Ancestors fed and seated at nature's table
were housed in her shade, warmed by a sun
not traded by any broker

Ring the bell this morning, top off the portfolios
downward red lines lead to waiting foodlines
and scraps withheld from dog tired workers

Pulling against their chains
anchored to a shore drowning in petrol rainbows
we are taught to waste rather than create

Responses are mixed at the pump
indexed and rolled into our 401k
shale that'll never shelter the homeless

At a precipice we stepped to, to feed a beast

monstrous air hangs by a noose around our neck
and now we scratch at a hole in earth's ceiling

Bouillon and barrels, our national treasures
can't cash in on bedtime stories
on love's market value

This slick business underfoot
pushes earth to an edge
and we won't stop stepping

Bootstrap

Pulled to fraying
Stitching loosed, a cycle and
A shoestring are keeping food on a sparse table.
Chin up. She only bows before Jesus.

Strung out on 80 hours,
With blisters and subservient nods,
Her keeping is on the dole
Canned, timed, carded.

Clocked hands and capitalism spin hamsters on a wheel
Pedaling pennies into other pockets.
Hand out dear. Pull on those loops sewn poorly
By investors in broken bootstraps.

Broken Wing

A nest, a home, was carried off a
ledge that a city had no good hold of.
Promise painted in eggshell white, was broken.
Beaked curiosity still searches for meaning in a
wingspan. Rebuilding from
survival and muscle memory,
with no perch secure, this promise will break
again in a thousand unnoticed ways.

Mourning

Autumn caresses this August morning
A leaf's edge whispers farewell to summer's sun.
Machinery hums on the streets below
Fresh mown clippings, blow about.
Man moves nature's confetti
until the wind has her way.

A mourning dove
abandoned her eggs in the oregano.
She returns to sip at the bath.
Miles away an ocean waves.
A gull and penguin take to different waters
Swept by wind and current.

Clouds amass atop rocky peaks.
Sunbaked earth cracks and dust settles.
Lava forces new formations
In rebirth and scorched forests.
A riverbed tells our stories in skeletal remains.

Global distance closes as my mind travels
Over Mother's gift this morning
And returns to an Ohio sun, rising on a rooftop.

Two house sparrows sing at the bath.
Searching, the dove returns. She paces
And cannot remember what she forgot.

Quiet with the dog's nose twitching
Goose flesh feels the coming winter with certainty.
Somewhere a blue whale's titan fin slaps cerulean.
Somewhere an eggshell cracks open.
A season of leaving returns.

Beyond Monsters

Half asleep in the darkened room, a leg spasm or flash of head-lights alters the otherwise unaltered space and I am left charged and changed
-aware.
Steadily a sleeper breathes beside me.
I may be the only one awake at this ungodly hour.

Poe's hour.
Darkness's friendliest hour.

A presence lingers in the room, someone or something, there.

The nightly chorus creaks, pops and hisses air venting a discordant song.
An old house calls me to attend its unnatural tones.
A rousing introduction, alluding to the intruders, Caspers and poltergeists waiting in the wings.

Soon, I convince myself I'm being watched.
- No, observed
and a faint shadow grows in a corner of the room or ceiling, where hiding spiders are cowering
much like me

cocooned in my web of a bed,
twisted up - too frozen to pull my exposed feet under the safety
of cover.

When the moon forces her way into the room,
eerily smearing her faint golden blue on
Antique White, we are both painted with horror. Silently still I
wait for a draft, a chill, a shift of light

a slight graze against piqued skin
is coming.
I must lay in wait inventing them all.
Brushing them off.

Peeling myself away from a catatonic state
I sit upright quickly, catching my breath in the
bravery of my act.
Daring feet swing, over what surely yawns below, waiting to
swallow me whole or drag me under.

I'm bold now, making mental friends with the monsters. Talking
scenarios. Negotiating with them in mind.
I carefully place bare toes on a cold wooden floor.
Spirits wandering nearby may now accompany me to the toilet
to relieve ourselves of each other and the intimacy of the last half
hour spent. I'm spent of fear.

Shuffling to the stairs I make for the kitchen light glaring beneath
the hood, leading me to a possible masked marauder.
Yet, only the refrigerator awaits
welcoming me as it does often at this hour.

Muscle memory pours my half cup of milk cooly into a glass,
the same glass cleaned from last night's milk.

Fortified, from the last bubbles of cream
I rinse us both clean of unnecessary remnants.
Beneath the tap a spell is broken.
A clean glass dries next to the sink.
I'm beyond my monsters, tonight.

Senryū

Yesterday was mine
Hot potato time machine
Tomorrow is yours

One cannot come inside
or step out of the rain
If one makes their own puddles

Pinot opened souls
poured into communion
stringing stories on vines

Spaces Sit Between

Spaces sit between us
The sofa gathers them with the cat hair
In her search for greener grasses

Sun strokes our fortune crossed by bad luck

Orbited by obligations
We tour guide two and four leggers through
Planets of pet dander and a Roomba

Screens close for the window at dinner

Sifting envelopes addressed
To two taxpayers over coffee or wine
Time litters its wrappers on our floor

Paper holds no sway over our commitment

Pup gets her rubs at bedtime
Cuteness calls off the chemistry and it returns
To our bed amid elbow books and televised tales

We listen to the things we read similarly

Home is full and we are filling
I'd have you for dessert again
If I hadn't loaded the dishwasher wrong

Warm Pairings in Iceland

Reykjadalur Hot Spring Thermal River, Iceland

In Embrace

After moon afternoon
Suns rise on our bed

Dawning in embrace
Sultry and safe

Flawed with perfection
Met equal, given whole

Timeless equations solved
With shelf lives less stable

Youth crept out of these joints
Creaking as time escaped

Still suns sink in our sheets
We fall again

Two Candles

One flame devastates me
The sad quivering of cold fire
Tapered into the finest point of

loneliness

Is nearly too much to bear
WhenI am awful,a solitary flame
Lit to better deepen the darkness
can steal all oxygen from the room
can snuff all brilliance from my soul
can notify fighters of my internal fire
No amount of dousing dims

isolation

My spirit is a twin. Yin to life's Yang
I am both light and dark
And must burn for it

Paris This Fall

My troubled mind wants me to write something pretty,
Lilting graceful phrases to counter the sweltering heat.
Singular phrases that may smother the darkness of our times,
In sauces so delectable I may forget anything unsavory.

Beauty and pain, both mix in the bowl between my ears.
Yet torment tortures my pages more regularly.
Filled to overflowing, both pour over my mind,
A sieve, emulsified into meaning,

In this bifurcated, bracketed brain, it matters.

Flowers, clear in the vase wilt gorgeously under my care.
Half full, the cloudy water of decomposition settles.
I love them, each petal, even after they fade and falter,
The beauty of knowing we all will.
Pollen and silky sheaths litter my counter,
A messy business, this loving.

The sun bakes roses onto my brick wall each morning,
My eyes wake warmed by the grey days too.
It is a surprising thing to be alive.

A cruel trick, a gorgeous one,
Played on or out, either way, a game.
Suppose its as probable as anything,
Including my death,
Which I hope holds off until after Sicily next spring,
Or for decades longer before she takes her slice,
If I may be so bold as to hope.

Travel reminds me of other lives, other bites taken,
Colors seeped into cobblestone.
Countrysides unseen by lifetimes of eyes.

Until I step on that thread of amber
Filtering through stone,
Until I watch that river carve her place in a city,
I command myself to live for Paris this fall.
Colors I've yet to see live there and so must I.
My sweet cat trembles in dream next to me
She will strike if I stroke her fur too long.

Towards

I'm running and have run
away

Witness to the scenes I flee
Captive and key holder to a past

I'm leaving and have left
pieces

Within future puzzles
Outside mapping points of light

Meteoric and slammed into walls of our making

I'm losing and have lost
myself

Champion of grief and victory
Conquering loss and vanquishing doubt

Atomic and benign in lethargy and action

I'm asking and have asked
others

Which way is redemption
Following paths leading farther than nowhere

Catapulted and crushed into bravery and beyond

I'm learning and have learned
the way

Growing on this planet
Siphoning minerals from my starry toil

I'm running and will run
towards

Myself and what nonsense will come
Littering and recycling meaning in these galactic bits

Undoing

The evening air glides over my tongue,
A chilled palette cleanse with just a hint of autumn
Reaches the back to my throat.
(breathe in)
My favorite season, savored -I fill up -
(breathe in)
And then take in seconds.
Though my breathing pollutes me
As microscopic unpleasantries suck in.

I, am the particulate of combustion. Fueled, from convenience

Still the sensation of filling oneself is pleasant
And distracting.
Mealtimes with my cage free eggs and bamboo wear
Tasty trans fats and glycerides hide in sodium,
Sugars and synthetics sneak in.

I, am a walking beaker of preservative. A chemistry project

Though with age, my very cells divide
With less ferocity than when I was young.
Sunsets arrive earlier after equinox you know,

Painting our sky in the beauteous shades of our filth
My sister has asthma. As a child, somedays I went to bed dressed,
in case we ended up in the ER

We are all dying anyway with or without an inhaler
In this great undoing of life
But there seems a hurry to kill each other
in awful and indelicate ways.

I, am the empath taking the side of humanity. Damn tree hugger

Can we live to undo
Or is the doing a done deal?
Can we learn to unlearn
Or is what we know all we know?

Our common stock feels less substantial
Poisoned by our pollution and an elusive peace
It eats away at our larger portions.
On our compartmentalized plates
Divisions run deeper.

People say they care about life
But they only mean theirs
Buying into caged eggs and their makers.
Potential- that is what's valued.

Social status rarely comes in counting others equal

I have no answers that will salve our wounds
I do know that stone soup is filling but

Sweets are always more palatable.

I, am wandering away from peace without freedom. A peoples
project

Older, we tend to taste tougher.
In this stew of uncertainty
I settle into the undoing of me
Craving the undoing of what's been done

Either way, apparently the sun will rise
on our wars tomorrow

100 Thousand Poets for Change -- Peace, Justice & Sustainability
- September 2022 participant with Ohio Poetry Association

Monday's weight

Monday's reality weighs heavy
as a distant land and a child's ashen tears rain down

How to breathe in safety that doesn't exist
For them
For me
For you

And I am asked to hate a side
Rather than love a people

Yesterday, pews were filled with silent hearts
calling on someone else to solve these problems

Today's excuses land loudly

Truth

I'm buried in it.

The telling and trappings of my truth. And yours.
I'm living proof of dying young from exposure
to my own cold and growing old
enough to know that one's truth can save.
I've warmed and chilled
and will dial that thermostat as I please
Thank you very much because
the world turns on and off for us all the time.

It turned away from you
and others who make us look
in the mirror and face the real demons.

You knew you weren't of this world...
Yet I'm not sure you understood
you were of a world many of us wanted.
Vulnerable. Exposed and exposing.
Cursed by an honest heart.
Blessed. We were. Blind.

A trajectory and snuff.
A glimpse of how hard we've decided
it has to be on some.
A Christ story, one of many we create and destroy-
you turned our tables and crucified our comfort
We cast blame for appeasement.

Gods don't treat us this poorly.

An easement on a road you'll never own,
yet you were never owned either
and therein lies the poignant beauty of our betrayal .
We cannot make something as glaring and wondrous as your sun
but we can burn
And we must burn in your lingering flame
And purify.

What's Her Name

Moss hugged a best-loved pot on my stoop, a decade ago.

What rests inside the gray, brittle clay, has lived through another winter.

Through the worst of it. And now, bursting through the chill, this winsome creature is threatening to return stronger than before.

Each morning this beauty wakes searching, in my dim grayscale breezeway, for a sun too far away.

And still she erupts singular of purpose.

I didn't keep the damn plastic tab to know the name of this rose colored flower, unlike any rose I've known, unfolding bolder each day. A bloom and three six fingered sturdy leaves reaching outward on a seemingly frail stalk, unafraid. I kind of like not knowing. Her name. Her leaves are evergreen, resilient.

Reaching into the waiting world, this brave beauty hurts my eyes and tears at my heart, for she is everything we must be...

Fair and strong, and able to grow in places that don't suit our needs.

Our struggles, unrecognizable.

This late winter morning, I found my misty voice singing her praises. Puffs of cloud confetti hung in that frozen air to later rain down on this this magical beast of a being, this unknown bloom, standing alone, daring to resist her environment.

This flowering warrior, marching well before March. More prepossessing for her struggle. How ugly, that we need to see beauty in pain.

Entropy

Stars cast a shadow even in utter darkness
Our clouds move past. The moon returns.
Are we the sages yet to see truth in tomorrow?

It is hard to care. Harder not to.
The fault line of concern widens.
A sprinkling of solution
Parches at the cracks in our vision

I am an acreage of resolve
Searching for a patch of sun
For my waterlogged self to soak into
our weather is fair or furious

My dog spins maniacally
Life holds us all in circling patterns
Devolving at the ineptitude of my words
Entropy barks back

Some people give up on things that become difficult
Coveting the blossoms of spring
My eyes shine brightest against winter's grey

Heart graffiti on mural in Reykjavik, Iceland - April 2023
*Photo Holly Brians Ragusa - Mural art by Skiltamálun
Reykjavíkur for Days of Gray film team*

Imagine Not Knowing

A fickle sun rides the sky on a carpet of clouds

An intriguing moon changes its mind

Some nights a shy star hides only to scream starlight at us on others

Each, steal away pieces of light for themselves

Science knows why

Numbers know how to build a bridge but cannot measure the weight of awe or mystery

Here, we analyze why storms rage and warmth falters, yet we can't explain why we bask in the glow of a snowflake

Here, where it is possible to get found on a backroads trail or get lost in the softness of a horse's nose

Making stupendous spectacles of ourselves, we know-it-all planetary shufflers, get off on regulating love and dance moves on this crazy spinning dance floor

Imagine not knowing you are the persnickety chaperone, trying to control the room

Sticklers, drawing lines even the Earth won't stand still for

Rules and laws, and all this knowledge and still we cannot measure the smallness of space a terrified child craves

Or be grateful for the many shapes love takes

Dissecting joy in the last crumb of a cookie

Imagine not knowing how to hurt another

How small do we have to feel to act big

How big is big enough

Class can you please tell me the standard measures for humility and arrogance

Imagine a world where one minuscule life doesn't limit another's

Specks, floating here, together for a spell, making a mess or making magic

All boats will eventually run aground, dry of tears or flooded

Imagine this short trip with a smile and without a chaperone

Imagine not knowing how wrong the need to be right is

A Lost Cause

I have been thinking about the cause of care
And when to know hope is a lost one

I was told recently by someone that it was
Lost

And the news follows up this line of thinking
And hard days seem only to confirm
How lost
How very lost hope is

Can it be found?
Entertaining an insane belief in a power outside of ourselves
I'm searching.
Not for a power of one or a power of none,
I'm not here to debate numbers, locations, labels and names
For where hope lives or lies

I'm considering the lunacy of magic and why kindness isn't a god and
My madness is multiplying how small acts add up.
How a tidal pull of tiny efforts creates a wave of humanity.

Unknown mysteries and natural forces hold doors open,

Press faint smiles into nods on the street,
Open hands and tighten hugs.

I spy the gale force of a tear washing over me.

I'm contemplating the momentous momentum of a meal made
    And love served piping hot
    With time and attention over a warm drink and eye contact

    Multifaceted these mirrored surfaces
    Seeing ourselves in others.

I have been studying the shape of a listening ear
    And seeing the swirls of loneliness there
    Watching the noisy view from silence

    Weary world, hot, exhausted, bombed and broken world,
    Are we hopeless?
    Are you lost or am I?

    Having been in and out of love with Hope for so long
I don't know if the toxic ingredient is she or me
    But,
    But, I give up.
I give up on giving up.

    And have resigned myself to stay lost
    And found in finding that spark
I spy a glimpse of it
    And have decided the color of hope is
    Not seeing life without it.

Wake Grateful

I wake grateful.

Not because it's simple.
I'm told I make it sound simple.

It is not.
    I am not.
    Though I might let others decide

Sincerity in an insincere world is punishment enough

Still I choose earnestness over sport
I'm not looking to score points
Cannot win in your loss or rise on your fall

I wake grateful

Not because I'm not gutted
knifed by regret, sliced by fickle friends

Friends are not.
    I am not.
    Should is a wasted word anyhow

Thankfully a tidal pull of gratitude flows

In this frightening, tossed aside world
Maybe we need to award more slack
I must wake with gratitude or not wake

Tilt a World

Squint to read the tiny print
on this manual of life
I was given no manual to live my living

No permission was granted
To become until I became the grantor
Think what you like
You'll be told it is wrong

Whether the weather is right
You'll blow back on what is left of yourself
And might be shot at the grocery anyway

Help cannot be heard over denial
Tell the truth that is yours to tell
Tell the truth dammit
Even as it becomes another's judgment

Hurt unexamined always arms punitive minds
We are gathered here to mourn facts
That died at least a decade to go

And to celebrate the immortality of lies

For God so loved the world that
He gave it guns and anger to teach us that
Sin was designed by men with money anyhow

My pew sits in moonshadow or a bench by the brook
Where creation reveals her wisdom
Beneath the altar of a tree

Settle into this brusque breeze of a fifth decade
Save your strength for the rest of your journey
Leave what crumbs you can
The rest is for the birds

Fervent thanks to my love, my partner in all things.
My life would reflect a very different hue were it not for the lightness of you.

All my love Mom, you are the gentle, bright sun that brought this bloom into being.
With deep recognition and love, happy heavenly birthday Dad.

Oh, two creative children, you humble, inspire and awe me.

A wealth of family, a treasure of friends, a cat and a dog with me til the end.

If we surrendered
to earth's intelligence
we could rise up rooted, like trees.

- Rilke

Grateful to these poet reviewers

John Burroughs, of Cleveland, is U.S. National Beat Poet Laureate, 2022-2023, and former Ohio Beat Poet Laureate. Author of *The Wrest of the Worthwhile* [2023, Far Queue Press], *Rattle & Numb: Selected & New Poems*, 1992-2019 [2019, Venetian Spider Press] and nearly twenty poetry chapbooks including *Dogging Catastrophe* and *The Eater of the Absurd*. Since 2008 Burroughs has curated several regular reading series in Northeast Ohio. www.crisischronicles.com

Jonie McIntire, Poet Laureate for Lucas County Ohio, is author of *Beyond the Sidewalk* (NightBallet Press, 2017), *Not All Who Are Lost Wander* [Finishing Line Press, 2016], and *Semidomesticated*, winner of the Red Flag Poetry 2020 Chapbook contest [March 2021] [re-released Sheila-Na-Gig Editions July 2022]. Her widely published poetry has been nominated for Best of the Net and Pushcart Prize. www.joniemcintire.net

Mervyn Seivwright writes to balance social consciousness & poetry craft for humane growth. Spalding University MFA grad, Seivwright has appeared in *AGNI, American Journal of Poetry, Salamander Magazine, African American Review*, and 61 other journals across 9 countries, receiving recognition as a 2021 Pushcart Nominee & Voices Israel's Rose Ruben Poetry Competition Honorable-Mention and 2023 Pushcart Nominee for *Residue*. His collection "*Stick, Hook, and a Pile of Yarn*," is available through Broken Sleep Books. www.clippings.me/mervynseivwright

Holly Brians Ragusa (she/her/hers) is an interdisciplinary writer, poet, speaker, community activist and author of *Met the End* (Nov 2022) which was named *CityBeat* Staff Pick Best True Crime Memoir That Cuts Away Sensationalism in 2023. Other books include *Dying to Know Myself In Time* and *Inverse; Informed Thoughts By An Unfit Poet*. Holly is a contributor to *Psychology Today* and an Opinion contributor to *The Cincinnati Enquirer* and *USA Today*. HBR serves a range of nonprofits, hosts writing workshops, builds bridges in community, and can be found moongazing in historic Over-the-Rhine, where she shares space with her husband, mother, three cats, one dog, and (sometimes) two grown children.

Thank you for sharing in this word journey,
Love & Light, HBR

Hollybriansragusa.com